Lot Casting

EliSheva Nesher

© 2015 EliSheva Nesher. All rights reserved.
ISBN 978-1-312-88833-3

Table of Contents

Preface

Acknowledgements

Introduction

Part I – Background

Part II – How to Cast Lots

Part III – Meanings of the Lots

Preface

The Primitive Hebrew tradition (aka AMHA) has been exported from its native Israel to the United States. As is true of all transplanted plants, it may grow and develop differently here than in its native soil. We are, as any healthy spiritual Path should be, a work in progress.

Keep abreast of developments in how lot casting is practiced by AMHA in the USA. Stay in touch with your class and teacher. Practice with them. This will help you retain clarity about what is healthy, natural growth and what is a fanciful side trip that leads nowhere.

This work is intended for the intermediate lot caster who has taken the introductory and the intermediate lot casting classes.

Acknowledgments

This book could never have been written if it were not for the 2013/14 lot casting class. They made me do it! And I am very grateful.

Bill Bulloch, Kenn Day, Shawn Dougherty, Brandi Patchan, Myrna Schutzbank, Sandra Small, and Chris Wallhausser are all the root of this.

And this is how they did it; Sandra Small suggested they collect all the notes taken as I was teaching the intermediate lot casting class, because, she said, I should make a book. Now, I had been told this before, but Sandra actually suggested a deadline. All of a sudden, I realized I really had to do this.

The class graduates all took time out of their busy lives to look their notes over. They complied with Sandra's deadline and sent her the extensive and lovingly-taken notes which they had taken all through the eleven-week intermediate lot casting course.

Sandra edited and collated, and sent their hard work to me.

All I had left to do was to simply edit for content, which took a lot longer than it should have...

Then Shawn, with great skill, patience and forbearance, edited what I had edited. Believe me, it needed it. Lastly, Kenn Day helped birth the physical product.

So, my thanks to all. You made it possible.

In gratitude and appreciation,

EliSheva, Shophet

Introduction

There are, to my knowledge, no people of antiquity that did not have a system of divination.

In tribal groupings around the world, to this day, certain individuals operate as Seers. Sometimes it is the elder women of the family or clan; elders of either sex; such religious specialists as "cunning men" or cunning women"; *curanderas*; *Babalaos*; shamans; "good witches"; priestesses or priests.

So it was in ancient Israel. Some Hebrew Bible texts refer to Seers and Seeresses in the Hebrew world who practiced a variety of types of divination. In early days the practice was held in such high esteem that even chieftains or kings asked their counsel. Consider the Wisewoman of En Dor, and Samuel, whom Saul consulted to help find a donkey of his father's herd. Or consider even Hulda, the prophetess, whom the priests consulted to ask if their text (Deuteronomy), so conveniently found in the Temple cellars (which supported priestly attitudes, having been written by them) was legitimate. This respect for diviners and divination changed over time for political reasons.

This world I describe, the world of ancient Hebrew divination, is not the world of the rabbis as we know it today, but the much older Hebrew world that preceded it. There was a time when the Hebrews were, according to modern secular scholars, not monotheists like modern Christians, Moslems or rabbinical Jews, but were instead, "Yahwist polytheist."

We know from the Hebrew Bible that in those times there existed sacred locations, like the oak grove of Mamre, where even Abraham went to, "ask of the God," i.e. talk to God or, as construed by some secular scholars, to seek divination in that sacred place.

Then politics began to influence the world. We know from both the Hebrew Bible and modern secular scholars that, at some point in history, sanctuaries and high places at the country's periphery and in more remote locations were closed. This may have been an attempt to gather power in the center and to concentrate it in the king and the temple. Practicing religion there was discouraged, or even forbidden.

Divination, although hitherto presumably practiced locally, was forbidden. What was later described as, "combatting polytheism", or "foreign Gods," was, in historic reality, done in order to centralize power, breaking the power of the clans and of the local priests in order to strengthen the monarchy and priesthood in Jerusalem. But divination per se was not forbidden, despite common opinion. It was now reserved for approved users. This is evidenced by the fact that the priest in the Temple of Jerusalem continued to practice divination. For example, note the number of times pregnancies of important figures are prophesied. This may have been done with the *Urim* and *Tummim* of the High Priest. We do not know for certain what these are.

Some scholars hypothesize that *Urim* and *Tummim* are objects used for divination, like lots. Rather than using the letters as they are used today, the objects may have held symbols that allowed casters to answer yes/no questions.

Others believe the name refers instead to something sewn onto the priest's garment, perhaps a pouch containing the lots *Urim* and *Tummim*.

Indeed, of the many different forms of divination that we know existed in ancient days, the one that is several times attested to in the Hebrew Bible is the casting of lots. We know that divination by lot casting was still used in the days of the Jewish revolt on Massada.

Spiritual specialists of the modern Primitive Hebrews/AMHA still practice lot casting today.

Part I

Background

Historical background

The Hebrews were a loose confederation of warrior/shepherd nomadic tribes who, around 2000-1500 BCE gradually settled and farmed the area now known as Israel as well as parts of modern-day Transjordan, Lebanon, Syria, and Egypt. They included tribes of people who were born Hebrew as well as those who became Hebrew by adoption, not genetic lineage. Our best written documentation of their history and customs is found in the Hebrew Bible.

Contrary to a popular misconception, the ancient Hebrews were not strict monotheists in the sense of modern Christians, Jews or Muslims. Modern scholarship shows that through most of their history the Hebrews were Yahwist polytheists. That is, they put their tribal God, Yahweh (or Yah) and his consort Asherat first. All other West Semitic God/desses were valid, just not to be "put before" their own. The Hebrew pantheon also included many "lesser" God/desses and Spirit Entities of the family, land and earth plus the sun, moon and stars, and various types of messengers and warrior Spirits some of which are known today as Angels. These other Divine Spirits and Entities were not viewed as completely separate from the nature of Yah so their identities and exact jobs are still somewhat vague in the Tradition.

Divination in ancient Israel

Lot casting is a form of divination first developed by the Hebrews very early in history. Lot casting was a way to ask the Hebrew God/desses for answers to questions of importance to the family or the tribe. Its use is mentioned many times in the Hebrew Bible. For example when Samuel, the prophet, was looking for the man whom the God Yah wished to name as the king of Israel (I Samuel, 10:20-22). This same system was used in Joshua 7:14-20 when Joshua and the tribes were searching for the man who had kept treasure looted during war rather than giving it to the God.

Along with lot casting, other forms of divination are also referred to specifically in the Hebrew Bible: In I Samuel 28:1-24, necromancy is used when the wise woman of Endor is asked by King Saul to summon the soul of the dead Prophet, Samuel, for answers and advice. Later, King David's faithful champion and general, Joab, sends for a Wise woman from the village of Tekoah, in order to influence some important political decisions of King David's regarding his heir and first born son, Abshalom (II Samuel: 14) which illustrates the important role such diviners had in the days of the Hebrews.

Divination was not reserved for the use of kings. In I Samuel 9:8-10 Saul's servant pays ¼ shekel of silver to a nearby Seer (the prophet Samuel) because he needs his help after having searched for several days without finding three lost donkeys.

A more complex way of finding out about the will of the God/desses was to "inquire of Yah," which is a phrase that is used several times in the Hebrew Bible. It is often associated with being at, or going to a holy place, like the oak grove at Mamreh, where the God gives an oracular response to Abraham. This is not likely to have been ordinary lot casting by tribal elders, but appears to have required an especially sacred location, with sacred groves or trees and a Seer to help in the task of "inquiring with the God." In fact, lot casting is not mentioned in conjunction with that process, so other forms of speaking to the God/dess, and getting a response must have been used.

The *Shophet*

Before the monarchy (approximately 1000 BCE) the Hebrew tribes would choose a combination war leader/chieftain and Seer to lead them in times of war and to mediate between the warrior aspect of the Hebrew God, Yah, and the tribes. These *Shophets* (chieftains/Seers) were usually deemed to be able to speak with the God/desses using some form of oracular technology.

One biblical example of a *Shophet* is Deborah the Seeress, prophetess and war leader, who sat under a sacred palm tree, probably planted in a High Place or sanctuary on Mt. Tabor, which is named after her, and "judged the people of Israel." That is, in keeping with her title of *Shophet*, she spoke law, settled tribal disputes, and in the process, talked to the God/desses and led her troops into battle. (Judges 4:4-5).

In modern Amcha (Hebrew Earth spirituality) the *Shophet*, female or male, is called to the job by group evaluation and consent. This calling typically occurs after years of training with an older *Shophet* and involves a form of public identification/acclamation.

Like medicine men in some Native American tribes, the *Shophet's* ability to retain the respect and credibility of the people depends on whether their promises from the God/desses are fulfilled, and by whether their conduct lends credibility to their fitness for this function.

Three types of divination in ancient Israel

We know about lot casting from the Hebrew Bible where it appears to have been used in three ways. First, to get yes/no answers from the God/desses. The second way is lot casting for family and friends which is the kind discussed in this book. It is an every-day device that allows you, the family (clan) elder to inquire of the God/desses when the next course of action is hard to identify or when simple common sense or the advice of other elders alone is not deemed to be enough. Any elder so gifted by the God/desses can do this lot casting for their own family and friends.

The third type of divination is a public ritual called Seeing for the Tribes and must be done by a *Shophet*.

To resolve more difficult, painful or important issues, the aid of a *Shophet* is necessary, since it is difficult to objectively read messages of this type. In addition, special oracular techniques are employed by the *Shophet* that require a native Hebrew-speaker's fluency and deep understanding of the language, history, symbology, and poetic metaphor of the Am Ha Aretz culture. This is not the same as being familiar with the Jewish rabbinical culture or with Western esoteric lore or any type of kabalah. Hence the need to request of the *Shophet* to "ask from the God/desses," "inquire of the

God/desses" or See for the Tribes (if this is a large public ritual.)

What happens when you cast your lots

Lot casting is a ritual. The Hebrew ritual of casting lots connects you with the Hebrew Divine Entities in their various forms. In casting lots you attempt to build a bridge to reach Hebrew Spirit(s) and ask for their wisdom. Therefore a respectful frame of mind is appropriate.

Please remember that lot casting is a ritual that is intended to connect you to the Hebrew speaking God/desses only. Therefore when lot casting, do not direct your question outside the Hebrew Pantheon. God/desses of any tradition will prefer to be addressed through their own Tradition's rituals. So, if you try to Ask of non-Hebrew God/desses by casting lots, you are likely to offend both the Hebrew God/desses and the other God/desses you are attempting to address. Sometimes a God/dess from another Pantheon may choose to step in to answer your questions, but the Godforms have worked that out between Themselves and you should not ask for that.

The Divine Spirit Entities

People sometimes feel they need a special relationship with a supreme or greater God/dess and go only to Them in order to get "good" answers to questions. But the Hebrew God/desses have easier-to-reach, more familiar Godforms, some of which do not have specific names or even precisely defined functions. They are known as *asherim* and *asherot*, and are the greater Gods' and Goddesses' more accessible 'every day' faces. Experience shows that it makes more sense to go an *asherat* of your household rather than attempt to contact the Lady Asherat, the Queen of Heaven, for personal questions. In ancient times *asherim* and *asherot* and not the great Gods and Goddesses were addressed in private devotion. Your ancestors, household God/desses or local Earth Spirits will know you better and be much easier to connect with.

Before you begin your casting, decide which Divine Spirit Entity you wish to consult. Don't worry about getting the wrong Divine Spirit Entity. Stay respectful and They will refer you on, if needed. Any of the Divine Spirit Entities listed below are appropriate.

Ancestor Spirits

Spirits of Ancestors that you relate to in a special way (from any ethnic background.) Perhaps people who were influential in your bloodline. Spirits of deceased people you have known and hold in high esteem (even if not from your bloodline.) Other spirits of deceased people, particularly if dead Hebrew warriors (*repha'im*).

God/desses of hearth and home

There is a whole category of home Godforms used by the ancient Hebrews for private devotion known as *asherot* or *asherim* (words ending in *ot* are feminine; those ending in *im* are masculine.) These Divine Spirit Entities preside over family life, happiness, family health, childbirth and prosperity of your private home. They have nothing to do with your success at work unless you farm or raise livestock.

The Teraphim

A group specific to Hebrew bloodlines are the *teraphim*. These Spirit Entities embody the souls of known Hebrew family ancestors. They are protectors of family members and their household as well as bringers of good advice on family issues.

Land Spirits of Israel

Regardless of your heritage, you may choose to inquire of the Land Spirits of Israel (*elilot* and *elilim*). These Divine Spirit Entities are connected to the water, land, trees, stones, fields, desert, rivers and earth of Israel. It will be helpful if you have been to Israel or have lived in a climate similar to it. (If you are particularly asking information of an Israeli tree Spirit, you can call him *ilan*, or her *ilanit* which is the Hebrew word meaning both a Divine entity and a tree.)

American Land Spirits

You may also inquire of the land Spirits of your area: trees, stones, rivers, etc. In warmer climates the *ilanim* will prefer to live in warm weather trees of the kind you might find in southern California, or the Mediterranean. In colder climates they will reside primarily in oaks, cypress, juniper or cedars, but not in maples or other northern trees. These trees have their own local Spirits and you might wish to consult a Native American Seer for more information on them.

Animal symbols of the greater God/desses

One way to query closer to the High aspect of the God/desses, without bothering the God/desses, themselves, is to ask of the spirit of their animal symbols, such as a lioness, antelope or dove (Asherat), a lion, scorpion or horse for Anat; a male lion or an ostrich for Yah in his aspect of Lord of the Desert Beasts. Note that the male lion can be a symbol for either Yah or Asherat. The 'lesser' Divine Spirit Entities do not have companion animals.

Part II

How to Cast Lots

Hebrew Lot Casting, as it is practiced today

In many groups of alternative spirituality, we hear of people who have learned a given divination method at the feet of teachers who may go back millennia, as far as the Neolithic, and their modern knowledge of it comes to them in an unbroken line.

We make no such claim. Spiritually speaking, we reconnect to the ancients in pre-rabbinical Israel. When the modern method of lot casting arose is a matter for debate. Some estimate that this occurred in the late 1800s of this era, when some small groups in Israel began to try to spiritually reconstruct and spiritually reconnect to the days of our ancient, pre-rabbinical, Hebrew Ancestors.

Either way, the letters themselves have traditionally been held to have power. Rabbinical mystics have held that they are sacred because they were given by the Divine. The letter *He* is especially sacred because it is used as a term for God in the sacred texts.

Letters were so highly regarded in rabbinical Judaism that the Kabbalist mystics wrote of seeing, in meditation, the letters burn and rise from the scrolls of the Torah like black flames arising to the heavens.

Therefore, lot casting today is, as in ancient times, a theurgy. That is to say, it is a religious/spiritual rite, as it is held to be a method of divination that involves, in fact requires, connection with God(s). The assumption, therefore, is that the Seer performs a lot casting with reverence for the sacred. That is, asking of the God(s) is a ceremony to be performed in a state of spiritual trance. In that altered state of consciousness, the Seer goes to the liminal places of Spirit/Gods/Goddesses, who offer answers to the questions that the Seer asks, usually on behalf of someone else.

One interesting aspect of the lots is that they are held to be the voice(s) of the God(s) and ancestors...of the sacred in its many forms. Therefore, they are never mean. They never lie to you or deceive you in any way, especially when asking of the ancestors. Regardless of their character in life, they have your best interests at heart. They have your back, always.
Therefore, lot casting is an act pertaining to the sacred. Each time you

begin a casting, you begin a ritual. You create sacred space with your intention to connect to Spirit.

It also follows that you can disagree with what you are told. In that event, consult another reputable Seer.

You do not need to be a Hebrew speaker to cast lots. However, you need to know the lots well enough that you do not need to refer to your notes or a book to know what each lot means. Having to do that interferes with your focus and interrupts your connection with the sacred.

Since lot casting is done is a spirit of reverence, it follows that when casting lots, the location becomes a temporary sacred space. Therefore, when casting, or in the presence of lot casting, turn off all electronic devices. Do not phone, email, or text, accept phone calls, emails, or texts, or engage in idle conversation. If you receive messages, excuse yourself. Leave the sacred space. If that is not possible, do not cast lots or put yourself in a place where lots are being cast.

The God(s), do not necessarily give exhaustive answers. Or perhaps we lack the ability to fully hear. This is where the Seer comes in.

In our tradition, unlike in many European traditions, the Seer is not merely a mouthpiece or vessel; we do not consider lot casting a way of channeling. The lot-casting Seer is a tool, but by no means a passive tool.

Tradition has it that it is the quality of the Seer's connection with Spirit that helps the Seer get a message and clarify it as needed. That same connection to the Sacred helps the Seer know how to fill out the "white spaces" left blank. This is, of course, where human fallibility comes in, and so it is good to be guided by ethics.

A discussion of ethics follows.

Ethics of Seers

Because we think of lot casting as a spiritual practice, it is important for lot casters to abide by some general ethical norms.

- Lot casting is a ritual. As such, you must pay your respects to the 7 ancestors and the tradition of the tribes. Refrain from behaviors that will offend them or the Gods.

- Do not ask of God(s) from other Pantheons when casting lots. They may be approached by their own Seers, in whatever other manner is traditional to them.

- Discourage questions whose answers lie in the phone book or on the internet, in a doctor's, lawyer's, or psychotherapist's office, or such. Tell the querent to consult human experts for the answers to such questions.

- Tell your querent not to blindly follow instructions from the lots. If major decisions are at stake, have them consult another Seer or other suitable expert before making any major decision.

- Do not cast lots if you are impaired. If you have a cold, or are not well, or if your judgment is impaired by your own emotions, or if you have taken a mood-altering drug, do not cast lots.

- Do not cast lots for a querent who is impaired, or who has mental illness, the ramification of which you are not qualified to assess, for example. You may not be able to understand the impact your words may have on them, and may thus do damage. This applies also, of course, to casting for mentally unimpaired people. This is simply ethical practice.

- Do not cast lots for somebody who is on the verge of committing violence to others or to self and seeks your sanction for that.

- Casting lots can be draining. Take care of yourself. When casting lots you are serving the God(s) and the person or community. While not a passive tool, as said, you are a tool of the God(s) when you convey Their answers. Tools must be well maintained. Take care of yourself, especially if the situation you have cast lots for has taken much out of you. Being able to access the Divine does not make you invulnerable or invincible. Some would say quite the contrary.

- Refrain from abusing substances of any kind, even legal ones. Under no circumstances cast lots, or do any other ritual from our Tradition, while intoxicated.

- It is especially important for a Seer to operate ethically in his/her life and to strive to maintain ethical attitudes and behaviors at all times.

- It is especially important to operate ethically when casting lots. You are accessing the Divine. Do that with purity of motivation. Casting lots to aggrandize yourself or to impress others is an offense to the God(s).

- When you are operating as a Seer, the querent trusts you. It is vital that you *never* abuse that trust. Their trust is a gift to you. It increases your ability to help them, and also increases their vulnerability to you. Do not abuse the authority that being the Seer confers on you. It offends the Gods.

- While casting, maintain your spirit of reverence for the One(s) whose counsel you are seeking.

- Approach the lot casting ritual only if you are truly free of anger or any other negative emotion, be it within yourself or toward the querent. If you are tempted to control a person toward whom you feel anger or disapproval by casting lots, you are perverting the purpose of lot casting, which is to ask of the God(s) and offer your best interpretation for the querent's benefit. Anger and negative emotion cloud our perspective and our vision, and casting lots when we are thus impaired is an offense to the God(s).

- It is important to remain as objective as possible when reading the lots and communicating the contents to your querent. Therefore, it is also best to avoid asking questions for yourself or for people you are close to. Small questions are ok. Momentous questions are definitely not a good idea when it is yourself or somebody close that you are asking for.

- There is a saying, "Be careful what you ask for."
  Changed slightly, this also applies to lot casting.
  "Be careful. When you ask a question of the God(s), you may well get an answer."
  As a Seer, it is your task to convey the answer to the querent.

- Cast your lots, and then pass on the message with integrity. Do not sweeten it and do not soften its content. However, it is your obligation to use enough social skill to be able to pass on the information accurately, in the clearest, most beneficial way for the querent. If you think your social and/or communication skills are *not* up to it, develop this if you need to, or do *not* cast lots.

- If your querent's question is a momentous one, judge carefully if it is your duty to ask the querent *before you cast for them*, if they are sure they wish to hear an answer. If they say yes, it is no longer your place to judge whether they should hear it or not.

- Sometimes, in very rare cases (usually only in life and limb questions), it is the Seer's moral obligation to refrain from answering a question. Most of the time this will result in the lot casting feeling "flat," or "dead," or it's meaning almost dramatically cryptic. If your connection to Spirit is sound, you will know when to keep silent. Say simply, "I am not given to offer you an answer."

- Do not cast lots for minors without their parent's consent.

- Feel free to reject an inappropriate question.

- Do not ask a question whose answer you yourself are afraid to hear. Refer to another Seer who has no such concerns.

- Do not ask a question which may encourage violent behavior.

- Practice clarity of speech. Speak in a way that the querent can understand. If you have to simplify your language to get the message across (for example, to someone less educated than you) do so, but never talk down to your querent. Remain respectful. If you do not know how not to avoid talking down to those less fortunate than yourself, learn.

- When reading lots, beware of over-interpreting. Read them first of all by looking and taking in their simplest, most concrete meaning. Lots are simple and powerful in their language.

- Read them right to left, even if you are not a Hebrew speaker. That is the tradition.

- Beware of asking the same question again because you or the querent did not like the answer. It does not enhance your understanding of the answer. Asking a question a second time to clarify a point is acceptable, as it does enhance your understanding of the answer.

- When the querent asks a question, make sure you understand not only the words, but also the intent and meaning behind them. The lots will answer those, too, and if you have not caught on, you will "miss" the answer's import. It will confuse you and the querent when you attempt to interpret what you have poorly understood.

- It is acceptable practice in some cases to cast again, with a different set of lots, if after several attempts you have failed to get a reading from the lots you first used. Better still, if the problem continues, consult with another reputable Seer.

- You may be a Seer; the God(s) may have gifted you with the ability to meet them in the liminal spaces and hear their answers. Yet you, and all of us, are still an ape that happens to have a soul. Remember this. It is true for you and all humans, and there are no exceptions. Therefore, acknowledge your limitations, honor them, and remember them when reading lots. It will make a better, clearer reading, for the benefit of your querent.

- Do not cast lots for more than one person at a sitting. It is tradition that only the Shophet can cast lots for an assembled group.

This may change. The Primitive Hebrew tradition has been transplanted here and it may grow and develop differently from how it was. But for now, this is how we like it to be done.

Deciding on the question

The Hebrew God/desses prefer to be queried when all other avenues have already been tried. If the answer is likely to be found in the telephone directory don't bother the Spirits.

Do the best you can in asking a clear, well-defined question. Do not ask questions such as, "I need guidance...." What are you looking for guidance on? "I need guidance in finding a job that pays $XXX annually," is a more complete and clear question.

Something specific about a relationship is better than a question phrased like "What should I do about Harry?" What about Harry do you want to address? Are you asking "Should I stop dating Harry?" or "Will Harry get a job within the next month?" (Assuming you are wondering if you should kick Harry out because he's not working and therefore not paying his share of the bills.)

The Hebrew God/desses will choose which of your questions to answer. Vague questions will just increase the possibilities of confusion. Warning: When in doubt about an answer (it doesn't make sense) check with a reputable Seer before you take any irreversible actions.

If you are asking about health care or a life and death situation, don't forget that there are plenty of medical and mental health professionals who will be glad to give you their professional opinions. Do not begin or discontinue medication or treatments without consulting them first.

The lot casting ritual

Begin with a purifying ritual. This could take the form of lighting some incense, or taking a shower and putting on clean clothes. Perhaps you have a special garment you will only use for lot casting purposes.

Burn some myrrh or frankincense incense. Use this burner and incense only for lot casting and nothing else. They are sacred objects.

Compose your mind to your sacred purpose.

Select the question you want to ask. Be specific.

Do not cast a circle. Ask *Ariel*, *Uziel*, *Raphael* and *Michael* in any order you prefer, to protect you, to stand before you, behind you and at your sides. Ask of one of the greater Hebrew Goddesses or God/desses to protect you above and below, (Asherat, Elah, El, Shekhinah or Yah.)

Spread the cloth.

Take the lots from the bag or box and place them in the upper left corner of the cloth. If any lots drop to the ground it is a sign from Spirit that the lot is not to be used in this session. Place it back in your storage bag or box.

The lot with the little sacred tree (a symbol of Asherat) on it goes on the right hand upper corner of your lot casting cloth. It will draw toxins to itself and ground them and keep the lot casting space pure (sacred).

Direct your thoughts respectfully (politely) to the Entity or Entities you hope will answer you and then ask your specific, complete question either silently or out loud.

Without looking at the letters on the lots, grab three from the pile on your left. Toss them on the cloth.

Turn them right side up and place them in a line. The lots, once cast, are read from right to left, as Hebrew is read.

For each question, three lots are cast, then read. Lots that have already been read are piled to the side and not reused during this session. Traditionally, one casts no more than three times, that is, one answers no more than three questions in any one session. The Hebrew God/desses don't like to be nagged.

When you have finished the third cast, say "the lots are closed, I have no more questions" and then thank all the Divine Spirit Entities for their protection and help. Don't dismiss the Divine Spirit Entities as in the European Traditions. Mid-eastern Entities are touchy and proud and will take offense at attempts to summon or dismiss them. A polite thank you and goodbye is sufficient. <u>They</u> are not leaving the sacred space (it's sacred because they are there and it travels with them), <u>you</u> are leaving the sacred space. They come and go as they please, they are not at our beck and call.

Put your lots back in their bag and store in a safe place with the cloth. Take a few cleansing breaths and then take off your ritual clothing and extinguish any ritual incense that is still burning.

Storing your lots

Keep your lots in a bag or box. You will need a cloth on which to do your castings. Use a cloth of linen, cotton, silk or wool. Please do not use synthetics as they are not traditional. Remember, this is an Earth religion and natural materials are best. It is a good idea to keep this cloth with your lots as they are both sacred tools. Because they are your sacred tools, never allow others to use them or touch them. If someone else touches them, rinse in fresh water and dry in the sun. Or, with the ritual cloth.

Part III

Meanings of the Lots

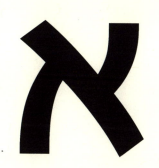

1 Aleph   Bull, (a symbol of El): the number 1000: a herd of 1000 cattle: riches: Chieftain, battle chief, and/or Shophet

> Aleph the chieftain
> One thousand and wealth
> Great Bull of Heaven
> One God who is kind.

Pictograph: Originally the head of a bull. Also means a "leader of one thousand, that is, a chieftain. Also, a herd of cattle; riches

Meaning: Aleph in modern lot casting refers to a chieftain or war leader ('Leader of One Thousand' was a title of biblical war leaders). Therefore, it can be read as referring to authority, or to chieftainship, or to a chieftain's personal characteristics. Aleph can also refer to a leader in the more modern sense.

The traditional tribal chieftain involved a measure of ruthlessness, so Aleph can show up as a warning against abusive authority, our own or someone else's. We believe today that authority may not be abused. Rather, authority is to be wielded with humility.

The authority of an Aleph, a chieftain, should be rooted in ethics and honor, thus fostering a sense of honor in a tribe, supporting a system of ethics that includes the traditional values of hospitality obligations, personal integrity, and steadfastness. A chieftain in the AMHA/Primitive Hebrew culture must have Leadership, authority strength, and consensus-building ability.

Today we read Aleph to mean that a leader, or person with leadership characteristics, plays a role in the querent's question. Or, that a situation may require the querent to behave as a leader, (that is, strong, daring or assertive), while remaining ethical, without taking advantage of other people's weakness. Kindness in a leader is a very desirable trait.

<u>Historical meaning</u>:   Aleph, the bull, was a symbol of the Good God, the "God of all the Gods" who was named El, the ancient bearded, benevolent ruler of the other Hebrew/Canaanite pantheon.

Since Aleph also means 'one thousand', it used to mean 'many,' or 'much,' as in one thousand men, or one thousand heads of cattle, and therefore implies power and/or riches.

ב

2 Beth — House, home, family, ancestors, lineage, bloodline

> Beth is for household,
> Your ancestors' line,
> All of your kin—those
> You are born to stand by.

<u>Pictograph</u>: Tent, house

<u>Meaning</u>: The place, people, or community where one belongs: also one's spiritual home.
The blood and bone of one's Ancestors are reflected in Beth. Beth can also include one's family of choice, one's "fictive kin" whom you have adopted, even if not of your actual bloodline. Beware, though. Beth never refers to casual friendships.

In AMHA/Primitive HEBREW Tradition: Beth refers to one's home lineage, tribe, ancestry, community. It carries a sense of belonging that involves deep commitment, and forms an important component of your identity. The sense of belonging to a Beth, (home, clan, or tribe) was, and still is, what holds people together and builds and maintains identity. Hence, traditional people do not typically have to "Find out who I am" or, "Find myself", as they know their place in their human ecology. Shared ancestry (real or fictive) gave, and still gives, people the ability to withstand adversity or hardship because it fosters cooperation and mutual support.

This is valued in the modern AMHA/Primitive Hebrew Tradition, as it encourages members to develop and maintain true friendships as part of a personal ecology that is rich with social support. This fosters human interdependence without compromising personal independence.

Beth can also refer to deceased family members, known or unknown, i.e. ancestors.
In AMHA/Primitive Hebrew Tradition it is believed that, regardless of what their character was in life, ancestors, once having passed to the

Otherworld, must have your back, be truthful to you, be protective, and stand by you. While there is a folkloric belief in malevolent spirits, those are never the spirits of your ancestors. So in spiritual work you can trust your ancestors as advisors, protectors, and benevolent entities.

Historical meaning: Unknown

3 Gimel   Travel, movement, transportation

> Gimel is camel
> A journey you face
> Go into Farland
> In spirit to grow

<u>Pictograph</u>: Camel

<u>Meaning</u>: Gamal, related to the name of the letter Gimel, meaning camel. In desert countries, it served most of the functions of a horse, except plowing.

Camels were ridden, hence Gimel means travel, moving from one location to another, It could mean a move to another place for the querent.

Gimel can also mean travel as a process of a personal, spiritual or metaphysical journey or quest (for example, one or more Otherworld or shamanic journeys, as a practice, not an isolated or occasional event).

Camels have a heaving kind of step, which can make some people mildly seasick. In the same way, the Journey or Spirit travel has ups and downs and is not always comfortably pleasant.

Depending on other Lots in a casting, Gimel can indicate a sharp or painful experience taking place during one's Journey, or as a consequence of it. Remember the camel's propensity to bite!

Camels also carried burdens, so a Journey can be heavy for the person undertaking it. Gimel is not read as any other type of 'carrying a burden,' only that a Journey of spiritual nature can at times be hard on the traveller.

<u>Historical meaning</u>: Camels made long, hard journeys across desert or semidesert possible. They were able to carry heavy loads for long stretches and did not need water as other beasts of burden did. Hence, their association with long travel rather than, for example, a shorter or easier trip.

T

4 *Dalet*   Gate, doorway, threshold

> Dalet is gate to the
> Places beyond
> Stand at its edge
> Or cross to the other side

<u>Pictograph</u>: Door, gate

<u>Abstract meaning</u>: Dalet tells you that you are standing in front of a door or gate, a threshold that is an entryway to a new state of some kind, such as a change in status or an inner transformation. Going over the threshold means carrying out a decision to enter into a different state of being, or stage of life, or degree of emotional, psychological, or spiritual development.

Very, VERY rarely, and only in conjunction with the other lots in the cast, Dalet may indicate a warning of potentially negative change, as in "do not step into that room."
If that is the meaning, the other lots cast will make that abundantly clear.

Most often, Dalet states that going through the door is an opportunity for growth and/or change. The threshold you must step over is not to be interpreted by the Seer as an obstacle. It is a point of decision…to cross through, or to refuse to cross through. The querent, of course, might be intimidated by that gate and perceive it as an obstacle, but it is not, even though there might be pain in transformation. Dalet tells you that you are standing at a threshold, that the time has come to choose whether to step through the gate or choose to stay outside.

Dalet in a lot casting indicates that the offer of transformation is readily available. A choice must be made to go through the gate, or to remain where one stands. The choice is to push open the unlocked door that Dalet represents and to walk through. This always takes courage. Even if one turns around and tries to go back out that gate, which can be done, the fact of having taken that step across the threshold cannot be erased and will leave its mark (usually positive) on the person and on her process.

Once you have chosen to step over the threshold, change can come in many forms, such as new responsibilities, or a shift in status. Examples include: an emotional shift from child to adult emotional range, as in moving from being alone to being of a family; going from nomad to a person settling down (but not vice versa, as Dalet is a door to a house, hence, to a more permanent state); single to married; corporate worker to spiritual healer, etc.

It cannot be said strongly enough that a querent whose lot casting includes Dalet can always choose to stand still, can opt to not to go through, and to turn her back on that gate. The lots do not encourage just stopping outside a gate and staying stopped. A person does, however, have free will and free choice.

Dalet also implies that the querent stop what she is doing and be willing to go through the gate of change and transformation, which in turn implies that she knows at some level that the door (opportunity for growth/change) is before her, and what it consist of.
The doorway always leads to something that already potentially exists beyond that threshold that has yet to be crossed.

<u>Historical meaning</u>: In the Temple, a door separated the public space from the space accessible only to the priests. The door, in effect, separated the inner and outer worlds, the here and there, from the world of Spirit.

5 He   Godform, Numinous, Great Spirit, Divine Being, The Infinite (Ayn Sof)

> He is for Spirit
> In all its great forms
> Soul of your Soul
> And the Wise One That Knows

<u>Pictograph</u>: Uncertain. Possibly, Man with arms raised

<u>Meaning</u>:   He refers to the Numinous. For some, this means the infinite, a vast, and pure Highest Being in its broadest, most transcendent, form, an entity that is so transcendent that it cannot be fully defined, such as Ayn Sof, who is Spirit beyond even godform.

In AMHA/Primitive Hebrew Tradition we think of He more as signaling the presence, or influence of a godform(s), "Spirit" as you understand it.

AMHA/Primitive Hebrews who are not mystics interpret He to mean the presence of the Sacred, in the sense of a specific godform of our traditional pantheon.
We may sometimes be aware of It being present, but may not always be able to identify specifically which godform's energy is manifesting.

If the letter He shows up in the answer to a mundane question, the querent will probably get an answer she is unprepared for, one that addresses the mystical/spiritual rather than the simple, everyday questions she thought she was asking.

<u>Historical meaning</u>: HE has historically been used as a substitute for the word "God" (YHWH) for those who did not choose to pronounce the YHWH word.
In AMHA/Primitive Hebrews we refer to this God as Yah.

6 Vav   Peg, hook

> Vav is the peg from which
> what is next hangs
> Things you let hang there
> Will hang there for long

Pictograph: Tent peg or, more likely, a hook

Meaning: Something in the querent's life or situation is hooked onto, or dependent upon, something else. A person's ability to move from state A to C depends on unhooking it from Vav, the peg.

Vav usually indicates that something can take place, but depends on something else the querent has the power or should move to change, but is currently stuck on or is hanging from that peg.

The Seer will interpret this to mean that an action on the part of the querent is needed. Sometimes Vav also means being too dependent or " hung up" on something. Either way, the message is, "unhook yourself".

Historical meaning: a peg on a wall

7 Zayin — Weapon, impending fight

> Zayin the sickle brings
> Barley and joy
> Zayin as weapon, defends
> Your own field

<u>Pictograph</u>: Cutting weapon, a sickle, a jawbone

<u>Abstract meaning</u>: You work with the land and it is your sweat that reaps the benefits. You may need to grab the sickle and empower yourself before you get the benefits of the spiritual harvest (abundance, joy, etc.). You stand tall, stand up for your opinions, and speak up. You may wrestle with yourself, even with God, but you have the courage of your truth. It is assumed that if you do this, you reap the harvest.

The appearance of the sickle in a reading implies righteousness. The querent must be willing to take a stand, even if it means God-wrestling, that is, respectfully arguing with God over an issue. God-wrestling is a Talmudic concept which means that you question and challenge rather than easily accept.

<u>Historical meaning</u>: In the Bronze Age, the jawbone of a donkey was used as a tool. The teeth were removed and obsidian or flint was refitted into the groove left by the teeth. It was used for cutting, especially crops.

ת

8 Het   Trespass, violation, offense

> Het tells of trespass
> Against your own kind
> Violates the body, the soul
> Or your mind

<u>Pictograph</u>: Boundary marker, tent wall

<u>Abstract meaning</u>: This represents a trespass against another person, yourself, or God. A threshold has been crossed without permission. In a reading, it means that the querent has been violated or abused, or is at risk of violating others. This violation will be crippling to the person in some way. The violation can come from people that you are with.

It can also refer to you trespassing on your own boundaries or values, that something that is right and proper according to your group mores or values has been violated. It can also be emotional bullying, or a warning that the querent is at risk, or is at risk of harming someone else. If it is against God, it is a serious violation of everything ethical.

If the violation comes from something your querent has committed, there is no guilt on your part. Is not necessarily wrong or something you need to be forgiven for. If you did something wrong, you must take responsibility for it. For every trespass there is a way to repair or undo the damage.

<u>Historical meaning</u>: In ancient times, property belonged to the clan, so it was never sold. Being a clan member also implied certain duties and responsibilities. Each clan member had obligations and responsibilities to the clan and, in return, could expect to be protected by other clan members. A trespass by a clan member reflected badly on the entire clan and, conversely, a trespass against a clan member was a trespass against the entire clan. This required a response.

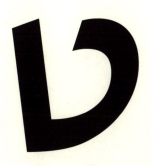

9 Tet   Strange, alien

> Tet is for alien, for what I
> Don't know
> I have not been there
> Feels too strange and new

<u>Pictograph</u>: Basket

<u>Abstract meaning</u>: Something strange, alien, or that has not been encountered before, especially in the spiritual realm. Because it is new, it may be uncomfortable. It is unfamiliar, something not seen before, and it requires contemplation. It is a challenge to your equilibrium, beyond the edges of your comfort zone. This challenge may be exciting, or may push you to the edge. It is neither positive nor negative, just unusual for you.

Tet can also mean a stranger.

<u>Historical meaning</u>: Unknown

10 Yod   Future, probability that something will take place

> Yod is for future, or things
> you must do
> Spirit commanding
> Saying "maybe" won't do

<u>Pictograph</u>: Possibly, and Arm

<u>Abstract meaning</u>: Usually shows up when querent asks a question about the future. It therefore stands for something that *possibly* will, might, or could happen in the future. It bases its prediction on an presently existing life pattern, which may be described by the other letters in a casting. Or it can refer to future trends or pattern.

In the AMHA view, however, Yod does not predict a specific event or occurrence because the future is a series of crossroads, and one's choices constantly change what that future is. So Yod is to be read by the Seer as "This *may* happen," not "This *will* happen." Hence, a reading related to the future can only describe what would happen if nothing else that is present ever changes, which is clearly almost impossible in human life. This is why future prediction is rarely, if ever, how modern lot casting is used.

Yod can be confusing in a lot casting because it sometimes, if rarely, functions much like He (see above). That is, instead of indicating something likely to take place in the future, it may simply indicate that a Godform is direcly speaking or involved in the action the lot casting describes.

The experienced and mature will Know (cap intentional) if the Yod in her casting feels like it comes from "Someone." As noted, this happens more often when the letter He is cast. As to the Seer feeling a Presence, this can and does happen in lot castings without the presence of Yod at all.

If the Seer Knows that Yod in a casting refers to a godform, the message may be from any deity, whether from the querent's tradition or from a godform from the AMHA Tradition, or from an unspecified but major Spirit energy.

The only exception is the Merman God, Dagon (#14), who is represented by the letter Nun. No other letter *ever* refers to Dagon.

Either way, Yod, like the letter He, can indicate the direct intervention of the Divine in the lot casting. Again, the Seer will know if this is taking place, or if Yod in that reading is to be interpreted as an indication of future patterns. When in doubt, consult with another Seer or with the Shophet, if possible.

<u>Historical meaning</u>: In modern Hebrew, verbs that refer to the future start with Yod. This is not so in ancient Hebrew. Hence, Yod is interpreted as possible future situations. Also,
because Yahweh starts with Yod, the interpretation that any Godform is involved is sometimes made.

11 Kaf   The cupped hand

> Kaf is the palm that holds
> Blessings and gifts
> Take what is given, let
> Rich blessings flow

<u>Pictograph</u>: Cupped hand, open palm

<u>Abstract meaning</u>: The cupped hand is ready to pour down blessings. Gifts are being offered. A gift is waiting to be poured out into the querent's receiving hand. The querent, of course, would do well to cup her hand in return, to actively accept and receive the gifts. Just standing there and waiting for gifts to pour down on one is not going to get the gifts delivered. That is, blessing comes from the positive action taken to receive it.

While one may not always identify something coming from on High as a gift at the time in which it is given, Kaf is never associated with impending evil gifts or punishment.
A broken arm, which is a misfortune, could turn out to be a boon if it leads a person to learn new information about, for example, climbing rocks safely, or perhaps to take fewer unnecessary risks regarding poor nutrition.

Make sure the querent clearly understands that if there is a misfortune, the misfortune itself is not the blessing, nor does misfortune *cause* the blessing from the cupped hand from on High. in AMHA /Primitive Hebrew Tradition suffering as such is not a blessing.
If we do have misfortune or suffering, it is our willingness to receive blessings despite that, or our ability to learn from unfortunate experiences, or the positive action taken as a result, that brings the blessing from the cupped hand. Misfortune only offers a possibility for transformation. It does not cause it without the participation of the sufferer.
Certainly, gifts also occur without misfortune.

Depending on what the lots are saying, a gift may be pending, but not immediate.

<u>Historical background</u>: In more primitive times, misfortune was construed as cause and effect. "I was bad, hence the God(s) now cause me to have bad

luck." OR, "I was good, hence the God(S) bring good luck". While we may wish we could still have that childlike belief, in AMHA/Primitive Hebrew culture we do not see things to be this simple.

12 Lamed   To learn, book learning, learned person

> Lamed is learning or one
> Who does so
> Points to the places
> Your learning must go

<u>Pictograph</u>: Unsure. Perhaps a Shepherd staff

<u>Abstract meaning</u>: The word Lamed in Hebrew is related to the verb Learning.
The querent is invited by the lots to study or to become better informed on a topic, to get more information from a good source (person/expert or resource/book, internet).

Lamed in a casting means, "Do your homework, or groundwork." Find out more before deciding." Or, "Learn to pay attention to what this is all about." "Discover the practical application."

Depending on the other lots in the cast, Lamed may sometimes suggest that the querent will eventually be capable of teaching what she needs to learn.

Lamed encourages further intellectual and spiritual development. Other letters in the casting may point to places where one's learning may occur.

<u>Historical meaning</u>: Learning from elders, which was the traditional way, was considered a good thing. Ancestors' function was to share their knowledge and experience, which was seen as helpful. More learning was assumed to mean one could be a better person, with more fulfilled potential, or could be better-informed while moving through life.

13 Mem   **Water, Depth**

                Mem is like maym

                Its waters are Deep

                Under its waves there are

                Secrets to keep

<u>Pictograph</u>: Water

<u>Abstract meaning</u>: Mem is, first and foremost, water, the waters of the deep. As with the deep, it can indicate that something is hidden. When Mem shows up in a casting it may be a suggestion to look below the surface. In a lot casting, Mem invites the querent to look deeper, to go deeper into an issue, or into the Self.

When Mem signifies the depth of the Soul, this is strictly personal and relates to the depth of <u>your</u> soul. However, if it appears with Bet, it may relate to your house, household or the Soul of your lineage.

Mem can also refer to the qualities of water, like flow.

Less frequently, Mem may indicate that something is thirsted for, or that a thirst will be slaked.

<u>Historical meaning</u>: The Hebrews considered themselves to have three souls. One dies with the body and may or may not "hang out" with the dead souls of ancestors. The second goes to the ancestors and is reunited with the group. The third soul is rewarded for good behavior on earth, or is punished for doing harm. Or, in some other views, the third soul can be reborn into the bloodline, living side by side with the soul of the infant descendant.

The Hebrews did not believe that you were born tainted by the sins of your ancestors, and therefore had no concept of infants being born with the original sin of Adam and Eve. There was a belief in consequences, how one's behavior affects the family, the tribe, and one's descendants for generations. An individual's behavior also affects how the gods relate to them all. Therefore, 'I need to act responsibly because the consequences of my actions do not stop with me.' Accountability was, therefore, a value.

14 Nun   Nourishment of body and soul, Gifts of land and sea

        Nun is the Merman, who

        Gifts from the sea

        Land gifts he brings too,

        Both barley and fish

<u>Pictograph</u>: Fish (God), seed

<u>Abstract meaning</u>: Nun is Dagon, the merman deity, who swims in the waters close to the shore and holds a fish in one hand and a sheaf of barley in the other. These represent impending gifts of both land and sea, as in a balance of gifts. This can refer to gifts that bring the soul or self nourishment/nurturing. Often He offers these gifts to someone who is experiencing scarcity. The merman god's appearance in a lot casting points to an imbalance in the querent's life. Acceptance of the gift can help rectify this imbalance.

The Merman God cannot swim ashore to the querent, because his large fish tail prevents it. It is up to the querent to roll up her clothing, wade into the water, and hold out her hands to indicate her willingness to accept the gifts and to actively take them from Dagon's hand.

Therefore, the casting of Nun may also be a warning. If the querent insists on waiting to be given gifts instead of reaching for them, or if the querent is afraid of change and so does not wade into the water to get the gifts (that is, persist in maintaining the imbalance in her life), the Merman will swim away and the offer of gifts will be withdrawn.

<u>Historical meaning</u>: The Merman, the equivalent of the Mermaid, originated in Mesopotamian mythology about 3000 BC in Assyria (Iraq, Iran), which was, along with Egypt, a super-power. He was the god of the

fisherman. He was represented as virile and muscled with a bearded face and a fish tail which started at the belly button.

15 Samekh Numinous, Bliss

> Samekh is bliss of the
> Heart and the soul
> And of the body
> It is never small

<u>Pictograph</u>: unknown

<u>Abstract meaning</u>: Samekh is the state of spiritual bliss that comes from your contacting the presence of the numinous. Numinous here refers to the Sacred Transcendent – often a deity. It is always a powerful indication of the presence of a larger force.

Samekh may indicate that an ecstatic experience of enlightenment is possible for the querent, or even impending. It does not predict that the querent will experience sacred bliss, but can indicate that it is likely, usually as a result result of heeding the message of the lots. It can mean that you are on a path that is right for <u>you</u>.

<u>Historical meaning</u>: In tribal societies, there were both communal gods and private gods, and a variety of types of numinous entities.

Angels, ancestors, and godforms of various types were thought to be able to play a role in human ecstatic experiences. These could be physically or spiritually painful.

An example would be the encounter with the numinous in tribal shamanic initiations.

16 Ayin — Well, Source, Seer's Eye

> Ayin means well, and the
> Deep Seeing Eye
> Seek Seer's wisdom, seek
> Knowledge from High.

Pictograph: well

Abstract meaning: Ayin refers to a well or source, and is often associated with a source of water. In arid regions, wells were crucial to survival. Finding a source of water was life-saving.

Ayin means deep knowledge, or information from the depths of the wells of wisdom, and refers to the ability to have insights of a spiritual nature. It can also mean esoteric information which can be found in sacred space. Ayin, the Well, is the sacred place where human and spiritual spheres meet. To have that clarity, gazing into the Well, into Ayin, was required.

Ayin in a lot casting means that the querent needs to go to the wells of wisdom and there can find the wisdom she seeks. Ayin never refers to a dry well.

In a well the sun and moon can be reflected. Sometimes ayin means that if the querent focuses, a meditative state can be achieved.

Ayin can also refer to "eye" or Seeing eye, that is, to seeing like a Seer would see. It can also be a directive to the querent to consult a Seer.

Ayin also implies a strong duty to follow the advice found in the Well of Wisdom. When doing a reading, it is critical not to soften the essential message of the reading. It needs to be delivered with integrity.

Historical meaning: The well was critical for survival in early times. Villages sprang up where water was available, so the well was a center of community life. It was an oasis, a source of life, and was usually sacred. People sought insight by gazing at the water in a well.

A version of shamanic ordeal leading to insight also existed in Hebrew Tradition: there were archangels, including Seraphim, warrior angels who might have a flaming sword. The kiss of such Seraphim, it was said, burns like coals. If a human was so kissed by Seraphim, it "opened" her mouth and eyes, and she became a Seer of the Unseen, whose mouth speaks to, of, and for the Sacred. The knowledge that would come to her, while originating from the godforms, was said to be found in the wells of wisdom.

If a person of the Hebrew trIbes was so destined, and was chosen to become Tribal War Chief and Seer, (a Shophet), it was imperative for her to speak her truth at all times, and especially when casting lots for the tribes.

The requirement to speak one's truth applies to any person casting lots, because casting is an act of ritual under the protection of the numinous, the gods and the ancestors. Respect must be paid to the ancestors. It is essential not to offend the spirits who preside over the lot-casting and who thus play a protective role for the tribe. So the messages from the numinous have to be relayed with honesty and accuracy to the querent(s).

17 Pe — Mouth, Speaking your truth

> Pe is the mouth and the
> Words that it speaks
> It means speak out or
> Speak for or speak deep.

<u>Pictograph</u>: Mouth

<u>Abstract meaning</u>: Pe always represents clear, firm, effective communication, whether speaking, writing, or teaching. It invites the querent to step forward and speak her truth, or teach what she knows. Pe may suggest that she will soon be in a position to do that, OR that she should begin to.

The energy of Pe is always "coming out" energy. In a lot casting it always refers to the querent, who is being invited to speak up, speak out, or teach. Speaking in this context also means speaking one's truth. The goal is to impart wisdom, not to engage in trivial conversation or altercation.

Pe tells us that our words should have value and importance and must be spoken with integrity and congruence. Humor or jokes can be Pe if their intent is to convey wisdom or correct behavior without humiliating someone.

It is always dishonorable for a superior to crush an inferior.

<u>Historical meaning</u>: Speaking, teaching, speaking up

18 Tsadiq, Wisdom, Kindness, Righteousness

Tsadiq a Wise One in
One heart combines
Knowledge and Kindness
It's what makes one Wise.

Pictograph: Trail

Abstract meaning: Tsadiq symbolizes Wisdom, which is a combination of knowledge and kindness. If referring to a person it means someone who is filled with justice and warmth. She is just in the law and exhibits wisdom, benevolent kindness, and righteousness. The wisdom and kindness assumes learning…academic, heart, soul.

This wisdom does not need to be sophisticated. Wisdom is the product of the heart and soul. However, knowledge without kindness is not good. Kindness without knowledge stumbles lovingly in the dark. So to become wisdom, knowledge and kindness need to be in balance. When wisdom and knowledge are both expressed, together they are more powerful than when they are separate. There is El's, the good God's, energy in Tsadiq.

Tsadiq in a lot-casting may mean that you should be dipping into the Self and finding the Kind One Who Knows within you.

Historical meaning: Wisdom was highly valued in late antiquity and practically became a god. Sophia (which means wisdom in Greek) at one point in time, for the Greeks and gnostics, became a godlike entity with a feminine face. This was different from the Ancient One, the Hebrew God of Gods, El, who was known as generous, patient, and kind, and was therefore named the good God, husband of Ashera.

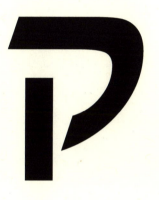

19 Quf   Monkey mind, mind which is never still (very significant)

>Quf is the monkey that's
>Trapped in your skull
>Jumps back and forth
>Round and round, never still

Pictograph: Unknown

Abstract Meaning: Chattering monkey trapped in your skull; unending thoughts which jump back and forth and go round and round, never halting, too busy.

Quf in a lot-casting describes a mind which is frantic, anxious, rather like the over-active mind of an adolescent. When Qof shows up, it is not to be taken as blame, nor as condemning the condition. Rather, Quf is to be understood as a warning that this agitation-prone state of mind is *never* beneficial to the querent.

Quf is a very important message to heed. It carries a strong admonition to pay attention. One would be wise to get out of this painfully tense condition as soon as possible! It is *never* advisable, nor *ever* beneficial, to stay in this condition.

This particular lot does not suggest what to do with the condition, but merely points to it. Explanations or further advice often comes from other lots.

Historical meaning: Unknown

20 Resh The start of, or need to start a new process

> Resh is the head or
> Beginnings of things
> Also means first, or go
> Learn how to think.

<u>Pictograph</u>: A human head

<u>Abstract meaning</u>: The start of, beginning of a process.

Resh in a casting indicates either the impending start of something new, or the potential for something new to occur, or the need for a new process to be put in place.

When referring to a person it means someone who leads ("is at the head") of something new. Here Resh refers to a process of some sort, and so, it is not to be confused with the meaning of Aleph, the chieftain.

Often Resh refers to the beginning of something new to which attention needs to be paid.

Sometimes, depending on the situation, Resh can also mean, "First, think about it," or "Go figure out how to think about this."

Resh is a neutral lot, and carries NO judgment of any kind. No shaming or guilt is ever involved or implied here.

<u>Historical meaning</u>: Associated with the rising Moon, because of the phrase, "Rosh Khodesh," which means, "Beginning of the Month"

21 Shin — Gird your loins, prepare for battle or challenge!

> Shin is the tooth and the
> Fang sharp and white
> It is soul's fire, hot flames
> Burning bright.

<u>Pictograph</u>: Unknown

Shin sounds somewhat like Shen, which in Hebrew means tooth or fang. It is also shaped somewhat like a styled flame, our "fire in the belly," or capacity for operating with passion.

Therefore, the lot Shin means "sharpen your fangs," that is, be ready to stand your ground. Access your power, prepare yourself, even (and especially) if you do not know that you are able, *go find your passion*, that fire in your belly, go reach for those abilities of yours, of determination, of courage, that give you the ability to see what needs to be done and to *do it*!

Shin may appear to be an exhortation to behavior raw and blunt, to acting with high emotion or power, but keep in mind that this is a value rooted in ancient cultures that still, to this day, *expects you to be capable of passion and expression*. In some cultures this was, and still is, much appreciated, while European style self-restraint can appear detached, cold and insincere in comparison.

Shin, therefore, may also mean, "Show your emotions. Be fully authentic. Act with clear conviction and be assertive." But speaking one's truth does not mean abusing others, so do not sacrifice integrity by disrespecting others when you speak up. You are judged by your actions far more than your words.

22   Tav   Stop, End, Bring to a close...and no hesitations!

> Tav is the seal that is set
> When all's closed
> It stops inaction and
> Action alike.

Pictograph: seal, as in the clay or wax sealing on a letter. Used to seal a letter, so no one other than the person for whom it was intended could open it.

Abstract meaning: Denotes the act of sealing, and the act of ending. It stops both actions and inactions.

The lot Tav almost always means a command to stop, or to discontinue something. It tells the querent about the need to stop something which needs to abruptly come to an end and be closed for good, *without delay*.

Tav carries a strong message, and the bluntness and abruptness reflects the sensibilities and character of the primitive Hebrew tribal culture. The reader/seer must nevertheless take on the ethical burden of speaking out on the need to stop a situation or a behavior with un-softened directness. When Tav shows up, do not make its message pretty or soften it.

"Stop" means *end immediately*, and must be conveyed just like that to the querent.

Tav may also mean, "Something has ended."

Historical meaning: Last letter of the Alef-Bet. Letters were sealed with a clay seal. Hence, the meaning of ending, of bringing to a close.